Family History of Hortense Patricia Allarie:
The Allarie-Dumas Genealogy
compiled and edited by Jordan Skipper, B.A.

2014
Winnipeg, Manitoba
Treaty 1 territory
Canada

To my Grandma, the elegant Patsy Schade

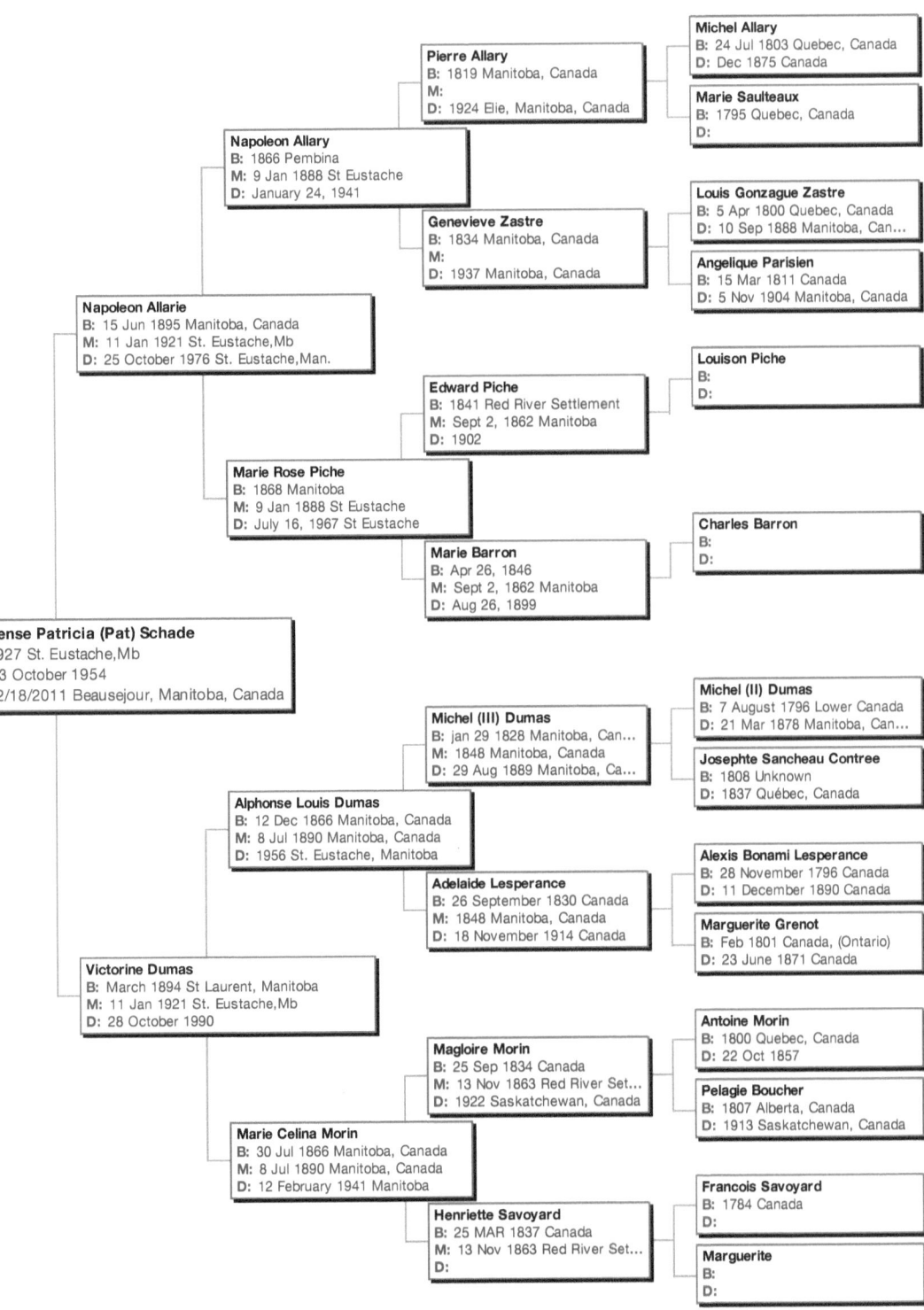

Michel Allary
B: 24 Jul 1803 Quebec, Canada
D: Dec 1875 Canada

Pierre Allary
B: 1819 Manitoba, Canada
M:
D: 1924 Elie, Manitoba, Canada

Marie Saulteaux
B: 1795 Quebec, Canada
D:

Napoleon Allary
B: 1866 Pembina
M: 9 Jan 1888 St Eustache
D: January 24, 1941

Louis Gonzague Zastre
B: 5 Apr 1800 Quebec, Canada
D: 10 Sep 1888 Manitoba, Can...

Genevieve Zastre
B: 1834 Manitoba, Canada
M:
D: 1937 Manitoba, Canada

Angelique Parisien
B: 15 Mar 1811 Canada
D: 5 Nov 1904 Manitoba, Canada

Napoleon Allarie
B: 15 Jun 1895 Manitoba, Canada
M: 11 Jan 1921 St. Eustache,Mb
D: 25 October 1976 St. Eustache,Man.

Louison Piche
B:
D:

Edward Piche
B: 1841 Red River Settlement
M: Sept 2, 1862 Manitoba
D: 1902

Marie Rose Piche
B: 1868 Manitoba
M: 9 Jan 1888 St Eustache
D: July 16, 1967 St Eustache

Charles Barron
B:
D:

Marie Barron
B: Apr 26, 1846
M: Sept 2, 1862 Manitoba
D: Aug 26, 1899

ense Patricia (Pat) Schade
927 St. Eustache,Mb
3 October 1954
2/18/2011 Beausejour, Manitoba, Canada

Michel (II) Dumas
B: 7 August 1796 Lower Canada
D: 21 Mar 1878 Manitoba, Can...

Michel (III) Dumas
B: jan 29 1828 Manitoba, Can...
M: 1848 Manitoba, Canada
D: 29 Aug 1889 Manitoba, Ca...

Josephte Sancheau Contree
B: 1808 Unknown
D: 1837 Québec, Canada

Alphonse Louis Dumas
B: 12 Dec 1866 Manitoba, Canada
M: 8 Jul 1890 Manitoba, Canada
D: 1956 St. Eustache, Manitoba

Alexis Bonami Lesperance
B: 28 November 1796 Canada
D: 11 December 1890 Canada

Adelaide Lesperance
B: 26 September 1830 Canada
M: 1848 Manitoba, Canada
D: 18 November 1914 Canada

Marguerite Grenot
B: Feb 1801 Canada, (Ontario)
D: 23 June 1871 Canada

Victorine Dumas
B: March 1894 St Laurent, Manitoba
M: 11 Jan 1921 St. Eustache,Mb
D: 28 October 1990

Antoine Morin
B: 1800 Quebec, Canada
D: 22 Oct 1857

Magloire Morin
B: 25 Sep 1834 Canada
M: 13 Nov 1863 Red River Set...
D: 1922 Saskatchewan, Canada

Pelagie Boucher
B: 1807 Alberta, Canada
D: 1913 Saskatchewan, Canada

Marie Celina Morin
B: 30 Jul 1866 Manitoba, Canada
M: 8 Jul 1890 Manitoba, Canada
D: 12 February 1941 Manitoba

Francois Savoyard
B: 1784 Canada
D:

Henriette Savoyard
B: 25 MAR 1837 Canada
M: 13 Nov 1863 Red River Set...
D:

Marguerite
B:
D:

3

Map of Manitoba communities mentioned in Genealogy

St. Laurent

Baie St. Paul • Beausejour

St. Eustache

St. Francois Xavier

Winnipeg/St. Boniface

Manitoba Act 1870

est. Pre-1870 Red River Settlement

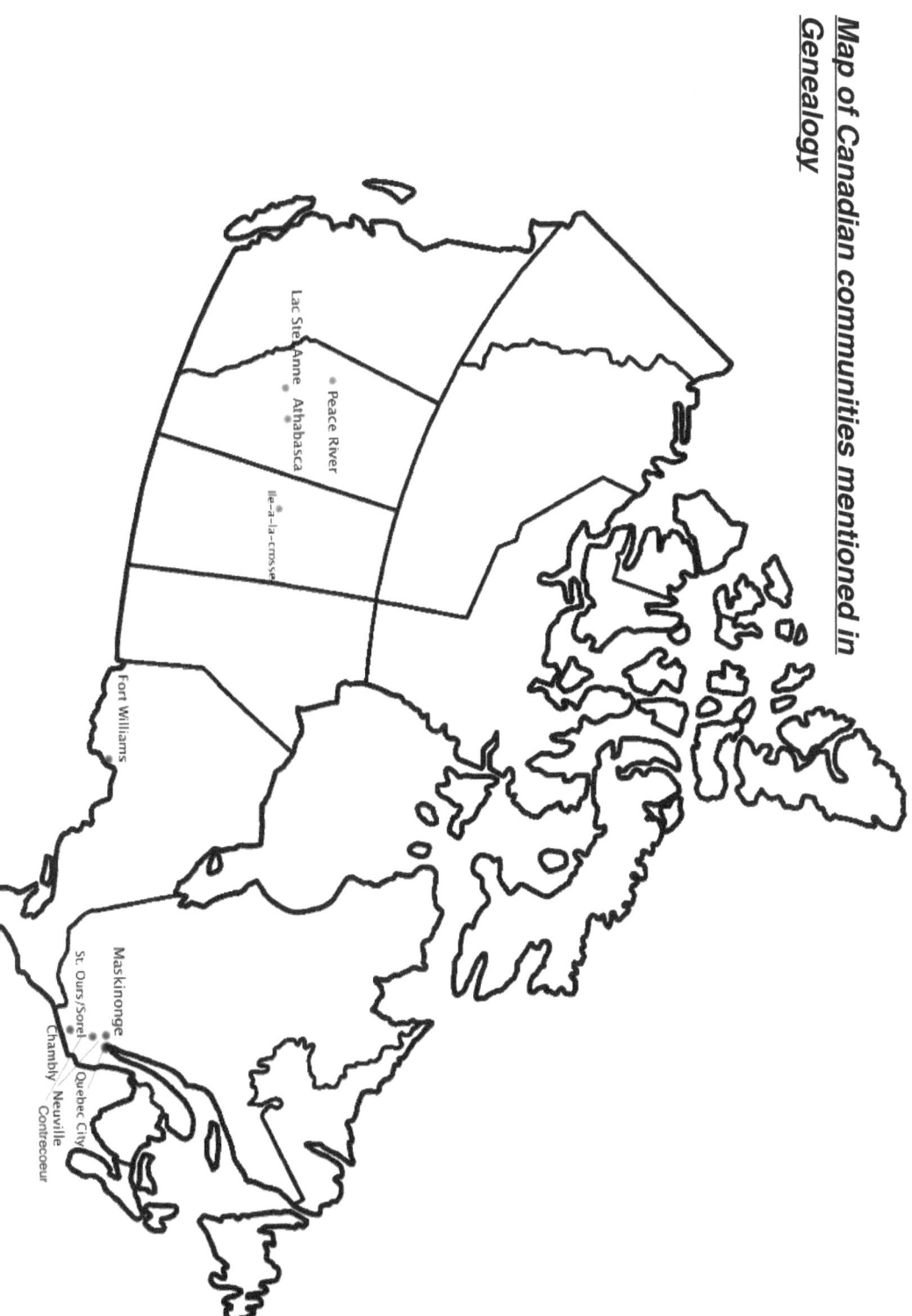

Hortense (Patricia) Allarie

(sp. on Birth Certificate: Marie-Hortense Rachel Allary)
Born 23 September, 1927 in St. Eustache, Manitoba.
Patricia's parents are Napoleon (Jr.) Allarie and Victorine
Dumas. Patrica married Herbert (Donald) Schade (b. 1931)
on 23 October, 1954 and moved to Beausejour, Manitoba.
They had five children: Douglas, Bruce, Les, Su, and
Gerald. They also have 8 grandchildren (Kelly, Danielle,
Nolan, Jordan, Kelsey, Devon, Ryan, and Derek) and at
the time of writing one great grandchild (Parker). Donald
passed away 5 February 2007 (age 76), and Patricia
passed away 18 February 2011 (Age 84).

Siblings of Hortense

Philbert (Philip) Allarie
Born 14 Janurary, 1922. Philip married Cecile Caldwell on
24 December 1948. They had three children: Denis, Linda,
Doreen. Philip passed away on 29 December, 1979 (age
57).

Alphilia (Alphee) Allarie
Born 1 April, 1923. Alphee passed away 21 April, 1982
(age 59).

Clarina (Claire) Allarie
Born 14 April, 1924. Claire married Alexandre Tetrault on
30 September, 1950. They had three children: Linda,
Edward, Gisele. Alexandre passed away 4 January, 1976.
Claire passed away in 1988 (age 64).

Simonne Allarie
Born 12 May, 1925. Simonne married Maurice Girard on 9
April , 1945. They had fourteen children: Octave, Claude,
Rhenald, Carole, Monique, Albert, Patricia, Sylvia, Elva,
Doris, Gail, Florence, Norbert, Sharon. Simonne passed
away in 1986 (age 61).

Arthemise (Mimise) Allarie
Born 6 July, 1931. Mimise married Gustave Painchaud on 14 November, 1953. They had one daughter, Joyceline. Mimise passed away 14 May, 1971 (40).

Valerie (Val) Allarie
Born 13 September, 1935. Val married Louis Arnal on 19 June, 1954. They had one daughter, Louise. Val passed away in 1988 (age 53).

Lucie Allarie
Born 10 May, 1949 and adopted by Napoleon and Victorine Allarie. She married Bradley Dawson on 20 August, 1977. They have two sons: Paul and Michael.

Napoleon (Jr.) Allarie and Victorine Dumas

Napoleon (Jr.) Allarie
Born 16 February, 1896 in St. Eustache, Manitoba. Napoleon (Jr.) was the third child of Napoleon (Sr.) Allarie and Marie Rose Piche. In 1917, Napoleon (Jr.) was drafted by the Canadian Army to combat in World War I, although there are no records of Napoleon going overseas. Napoleon (Jr.) married Victorine Dumas on 11 January, 1921 in St. Eustache. They had 8 children (See Hortense Allarie and Siblings). Napoleon (Jr.) and Victorine lived on the Allarie farm north of the village of St. Eustache on what is now Allarie Street. Napoleon (Jr.) passed away on 25 October, 1976 (Age 81).

Victorine Dumas
Born March, 1894 in St. Laurent, Manitoba. Victorine was the second child of Alphonse Louis Dumas and Marie Celina Morin. In 1901, Alphonse Louis and Family moved to St. Francois-Xavier (Victorine age 7), then to Baie St. Paul in 1906 (Victorine age 12). Victorine married Napoleon (Jr.) Allarie 11 January, 1921. Victorine moved to Beausejour, Manitoba and then Winnipeg, Manitoba after

the passing of Napoleon (Jr.) in 1976. Victorine passed away 28 October, 1990 (Age 96).

Siblings of Napoleon (Jr.) Allarie

Elzear Allarie (Born 1890; Married Donalda Richard 1909; Passed away 1952)
Gabriel Allarie (Born 1894; Married Armandine Tetu 1931; Passed away 1983)
Jean Allarie (Born 1898; Married Amanda Gregoire 1942; Passed away 1978)
Maria Allarie (Married Jean Millaire 1943; Birth and Death year unknown)
Raphael Allarie (Born 1900; Married Camilia Lussier 1930; Passed away 1992)
Julienne Allarie (Born 1905; Passed away 1906)
Damas Allarie (Born 1906; Passed away 1913)
George Aime Allarie (Born 1907; Passed away 1907)
Aime George Allarie (Born 1908; Passed away 1908)
* Two others passed away in infancy.

Siblings of Victorine Dumas

Alvina Dumas (Born 1892; Passed away unknown)
Mary Rose Dumas (Born 1895; Passed away unknown)
Evelsea Dumas (Born 1900; Passed away unknown)
Octavie Dumas (Born 1903; Passed away unknown)

Allarie Family Tree

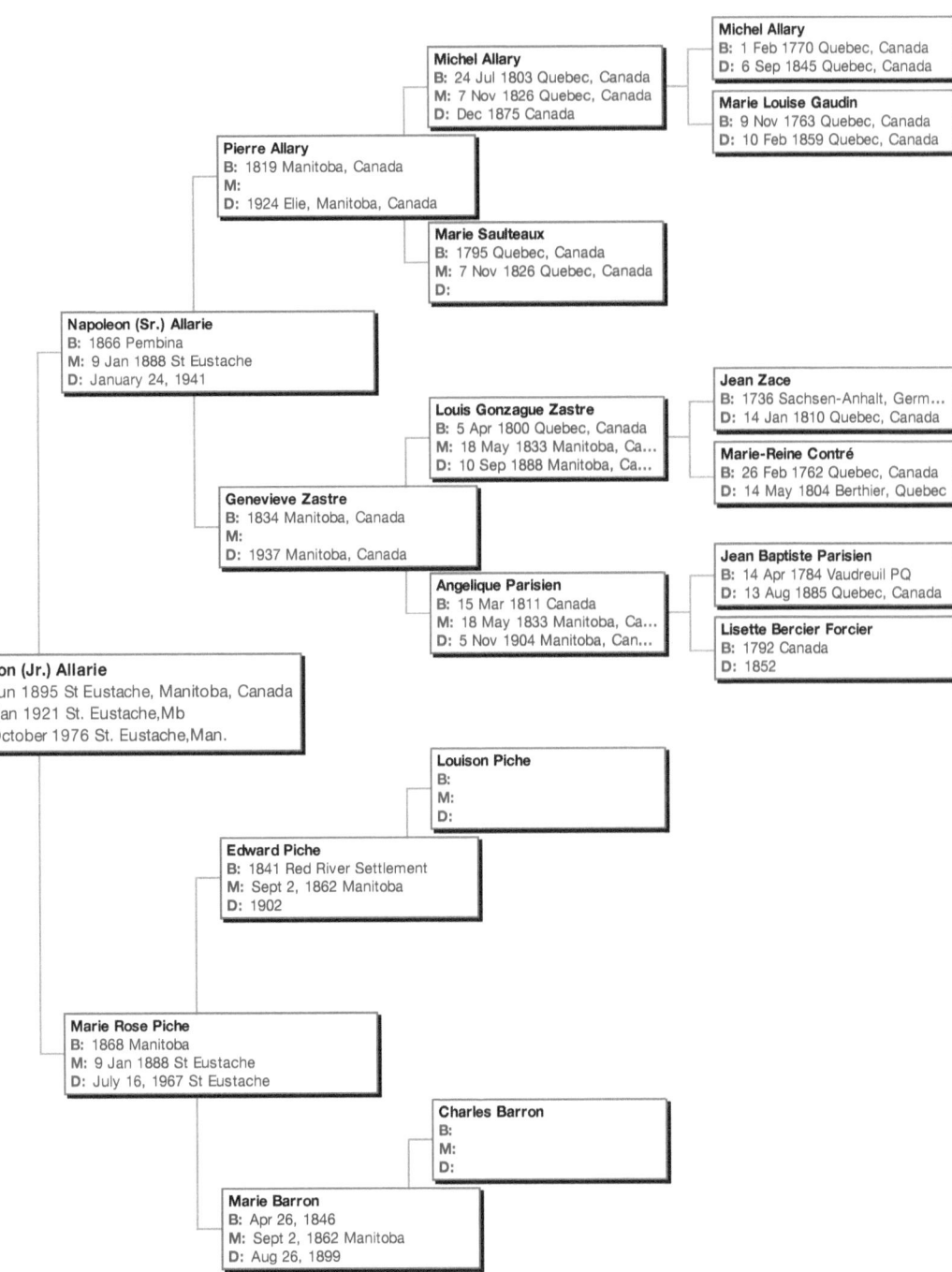

Michel Allary
B: 1 Feb 1770 Quebec, Canada
D: 6 Sep 1845 Quebec, Canada

Michel Allary
B: 24 Jul 1803 Quebec, Canada
M: 7 Nov 1826 Quebec, Canada
D: Dec 1875 Canada

Marie Louise Gaudin
B: 9 Nov 1763 Quebec, Canada
D: 10 Feb 1859 Quebec, Canada

Pierre Allary
B: 1819 Manitoba, Canada
M:
D: 1924 Elie, Manitoba, Canada

Marie Saulteaux
B: 1795 Quebec, Canada
M: 7 Nov 1826 Quebec, Canada
D:

Napoleon (Sr.) Allarie
B: 1866 Pembina
M: 9 Jan 1888 St Eustache
D: January 24, 1941

Jean Zace
B: 1736 Sachsen-Anhalt, Germ...
D: 14 Jan 1810 Quebec, Canada

Louis Gonzague Zastre
B: 5 Apr 1800 Quebec, Canada
M: 18 May 1833 Manitoba, Ca...
D: 10 Sep 1888 Manitoba, Ca...

Marie-Reine Contré
B: 26 Feb 1762 Quebec, Canada
D: 14 May 1804 Berthier, Quebec

Genevieve Zastre
B: 1834 Manitoba, Canada
M:
D: 1937 Manitoba, Canada

Jean Baptiste Parisien
B: 14 Apr 1784 Vaudreuil PQ
D: 13 Aug 1885 Quebec, Canada

Angelique Parisien
B: 15 Mar 1811 Canada
M: 18 May 1833 Manitoba, Ca...
D: 5 Nov 1904 Manitoba, Can...

Lisette Bercier Forcier
B: 1792 Canada
D: 1852

leon (Jr.) Allarie
Jun 1895 St Eustache, Manitoba, Canada
Jan 1921 St. Eustache,Mb
October 1976 St. Eustache,Man.

Louison Piche
B:
M:
D:

Edward Piche
B: 1841 Red River Settlement
M: Sept 2, 1862 Manitoba
D: 1902

Marie Rose Piche
B: 1868 Manitoba
M: 9 Jan 1888 St Eustache
D: July 16, 1967 St Eustache

Charles Barron
B:
M:
D:

Marie Barron
B: Apr 26, 1846
M: Sept 2, 1862 Manitoba
D: Aug 26, 1899

Napoleon (Sr.) Allarie and Marie Rose Piche

Napoleon (Sr.) Allarie [Metis]
Born 12 June, 1861 (1901 census has year of birth 1866).
Napoleon (Sr.) is the son of Pierre Allary and Genevieve
Zastre. Napoleon (Sr.) married Marie Rose Piche in the old
St. Eustache chapel. Napoleon (Sr.) bought a 37 acre
piece of land north of St. Eustache, Manitoba where he
raised his family. Napoleon (Sr.) also ran the Allarie Ferry
for many years. Napoleon (Sr.) passed away 24 January,
1941 (Age 80). The known siblings of Napoleon (Sr.) are
Jusue Allarie, Elzear Allarie, and Louis Allarie.

Maire Rose Piche [Metis]
Born 1868 (1901 census has year of birth 1871). Marie
Rose is the daughter of Edward Piche and Marie Barron.
Marie Rose passed away 16 July, 1967 (Age 99).

Edward Piche and Marie Barron

Edward Piche [Metis]
Born 1841 in the Red River Settlement. Manitoba.
Edwards father is Louison Piche, his mother is unknown.
Edward married Marie Barron on 2 September, 1862 in St.
Francois Xavier. Edward passed away in 1902 (age 61).

Marie Barron [Metis]
Born 26 April, 1846. Marie's father is Charles Barron, her
mother is unknown. Marie married Edward Piche 2
September, 1862 in St. Francois Xavier. Marie passed
away 26 August, 1899 (age 53).

Pierre Allary and Genevieve Zastre

Pierre Allary [Metis]

Born 1819 in Manitoba. Pierre is one of many children of Michel Allary and Marie (Gros Ventre) In 1827, Pierre married Genevieve Zastre. Pierre worked for the Hudson Bay company for 15 years. Pierre was an avid buffalo hunter, and one of the early settlers of the Baie St. Paul/St. Eustache region. Pierre was the first to operate a ferry across the Assiniboine River. Pierre however was one of the lowest paid ferrymen in the region, making $14.25/ month. The ferry, named 'Allary Ferry' grew to fame in the area; A local school got renamed to Allary school, as well as a road ('Allarie Street' in St. Eustache). Pierre was known for his storytelling, often telling newcomers stories about "the West", buffalo hunts, and the local indigenous people. Pierre was known in the community for being active all the way through his old age.

Pierre's Obituary read:

> One Dead Pierre is Dead; Sorrow in St. Eustache. Pierre Allary, 106 Years of Age, Veteran of Many Buffalo Hunts, Passes Away. Four Great Great Grand Children survive him. With the death of Pierre Allary at St. Eustache, Man., on Monday, May 12, at the venerable age of 106 years, is severed a tie with the early days of the west which cannot be replaced. Known to his friends and all who knew him were his friends as "le vleux St. Pierre.". A resident of St, Eustache for the past 50 years, and was the principal organizer and founder of the little parish of Bale St. Paul, now St Eustache. He was laid to rest this morning in the village which for so many long years had been his home. The pall-bearers were all pioneers and comrades of "le vleux St. Pierre" during the turbulent days of the early west. The memories of the dangers and thrilling

adventures of the pioneer days were fresh In the mind of "le vleux St - Pierre" until the day of his death. Often would he carry his listeners back to the early 1800's with his tales of Indian wars and buffalo hunts, when he was an employe of the Hudson's Bay' Company, for whom he worked for 15 years. He was one of the first ferrymen on the Assiniboine River, and for 30 years carried the prairie schooners. with their loads across the river and directed them on their way to the new west. Retained Strength Until three or four years ago, Mr. Allary retained his health and strength. He would walk four miles to church every sunday and could handle a gun with the best of the younger men. At the age of 27 years he married Genevieve Zastre, who predeceased him a few years ago. Fourteen children were born to them, nine of whom are still living. They are: Hyacinthe, Napoleon, Elzear, Joseph, Mrs. Alfred Lynch, Mrs. J, Brown, of St. Eustache, Louis, Mrs. Fraser, of Olga, N.D., Mrs. Desjarlals, of Togo, Honk. 70 grand - children, 41 great - grand - children, and four great - great - grand - children survive "le vleux St. Pierre."

One of the many stories that Pierre shared was the tale of the White House. The following passage is from the "Treasures of Time: The Rural Municipality of Cartier"

" Old man Allarie of the Allarie Ferry and his wife used to visit my parents. They could tell the old stories much better than we can today. The other man who verified this story was Art Boivin who lived across the river.

"On the south side of the river, near Headingley us a place where a creek drains into the Assiniboine. There was an old Hudson's Bay store there. The Old Hudson's

Bay Company posts were all build the same. That's where the Indians would meet, once a year. The tribe that had the Indian maiden came from farther away, Lac du Bonnet or Pine Falls.

It was considered a crime for one tribe to marry into another tribe. It was a chief;s son who was to marry; the girl was suppose to marry a closer relation. When they heard that the girl had married, this demanded revenge.

In the early days, the Indian trail angled across country about fifty miles. When the treaty was signed in 1870, the Indian trail was marked on the treaty. Nothing can block the trail, no matter where or how.

When the wedding of the Indian maiden took place, a gift had to be given. The White Horse was the gift that the from gave to the old man.

When they heard that the other bunch was coming for revenge, the chief gave the young couple the White Horse to get away. It was a very special horse, no other horses was known to keep up.

If they had crossed there at the big bend near Headingley, they could have got away. But they took the ridge, the old Indian trail. They were cut off by their pursuers. They had to turn off to the west. They had to follow the Ingleside Creek and just as they were leaving the Cartier Municipality, they ran into a swamp. Here they were massacred. They were both on the same horse. The two were killed but they could not catch the White Horse. To the indians, the White Horse was an evil spirit. They horse could go through the swamp where the pursers could not go and they could not reach him.

For many years there was a light that appeared there — a mystery light. "

"Mr. Allaire would tell that it was the White Horse. As you moved towards it, it disappeared or moved. The early settlers told of the massacre in that swamp, and many people were afraid of it. That light remained there until the big drain was put through. The horse was described as a fierce-looking animal and to the Indians it was very special. The White Horse, according to Mr. Allarie, never was north of the river."

Pierre passed away on 12 May, 1924 (age 105)

Genevieve Zastre [Metis]
Born in 1834 in St. Boniface, Manitoba. Genevieve's parents are Louis Gonzauge Zastre and Angelique Parisien. Genevieve's brother, Jean Baptiste Zace, married Marguerite Riel, sister of Louis Riel and granddaughter of Jean Baptiste Lagimodiere and Mary-Anne Gaboury (the first European female to settle in Western Canada). Genevieve married Pierre Allary in 1827. Genevieve passed away in 1937 (age 103).

Michel Allary and Marie Piik-siik-sii-na
Michel Allary
Born 24 July, 1803 in Ponte Du Lac, Quebec. Michel is the son of Michel (Sr.) Allary and Marie Louise Gaudin. On 7 November, 1871, Michel married Marie, and Saulteaux Ojibwe woman from Northern Canada. Michel passed away December 1875 (age 72).

Marie Piik-siik-sii-na [Gros Ventre/Algonquain]
Born 1795 in the North West territories of Canada. Marie married Michel Allary on 7 November, 1826. Marie's parents are unknown, as well as year of passing is unknown.

Louis Gonzague Zastre and Angelique Parisien

Louis Gonzague Zastre
Born 5 April, 1800 in Berthierville, Quebec. Louis is the son of Jean Zace and Marie-Reine Contre. Louis married Angelique Parisien 18 May, 1833 in St. Boniface, Manitoba. Louis passed away 10 September, 1888 (age 88).

Angelique Parisien [Metis]
Born 15 March, 1811 in the North West Territories of Canada. Angelique is the daughter of Jean Baptiste Parisien and Lisette Forcier. Angelique married Louis Gonzague Zastre on 18 May, 1833. Angelique passed away on 5 November, 1904 in St. Francois Xavier (age 93).

Michel (Sr.) Allary and Marie Louise Gaudin

Michel (Sr.) Allary
Born 1 February, 1770 in Trois-Riveres, Quebec. Michel (Sr.) married Marie Louise Gaudin 19 August, 1799 in Pointe-du-lac, Quebec. Michel (Sr.) passed away 6 September, 1845 (age 75).

Marie Louise Gaudin
Born 9 November, 1763 in St. Genevieve, Quebec. Marie Louise married Michel (Sr.) Allary 19 August, 1799. Marie Louise passed away 10 February, 1859 (age 95).

Jean Zace and Marie-Reine Contre

Jean Zace
Born 1736 in Magdeburg, Germany. Jean Zace married Marie-Reine Contre on 3 February, 1785 in Quebec. Jean passed away 14 January, 1810 (age 74).

Marie-Reine Contre
Born 26 February, 1762 in Berthiervile, Quebec. Maire-Reine married Jean Zace 3 February, 1785. Marie-Reine passed away 14 May, 1804 (age 42).

Jean Baptiste Parisien and Lisette Forcier

Jean Baptiste Parisien
Born 15 April, 1784 in St. Michels, Quebec. Jean Baptiste married Lisette Forcier in Alabama in 1826. Jean Baptiste passed away 13 August, 1885 (age 101).

Lisette Forcier [Indigenous]
Born 1792 in the North West Territories of Canada. Lisette married Jean Baptiste Parisien in 1826. Lisette passed away in 1852 (age 60).

Dumas Family Tree

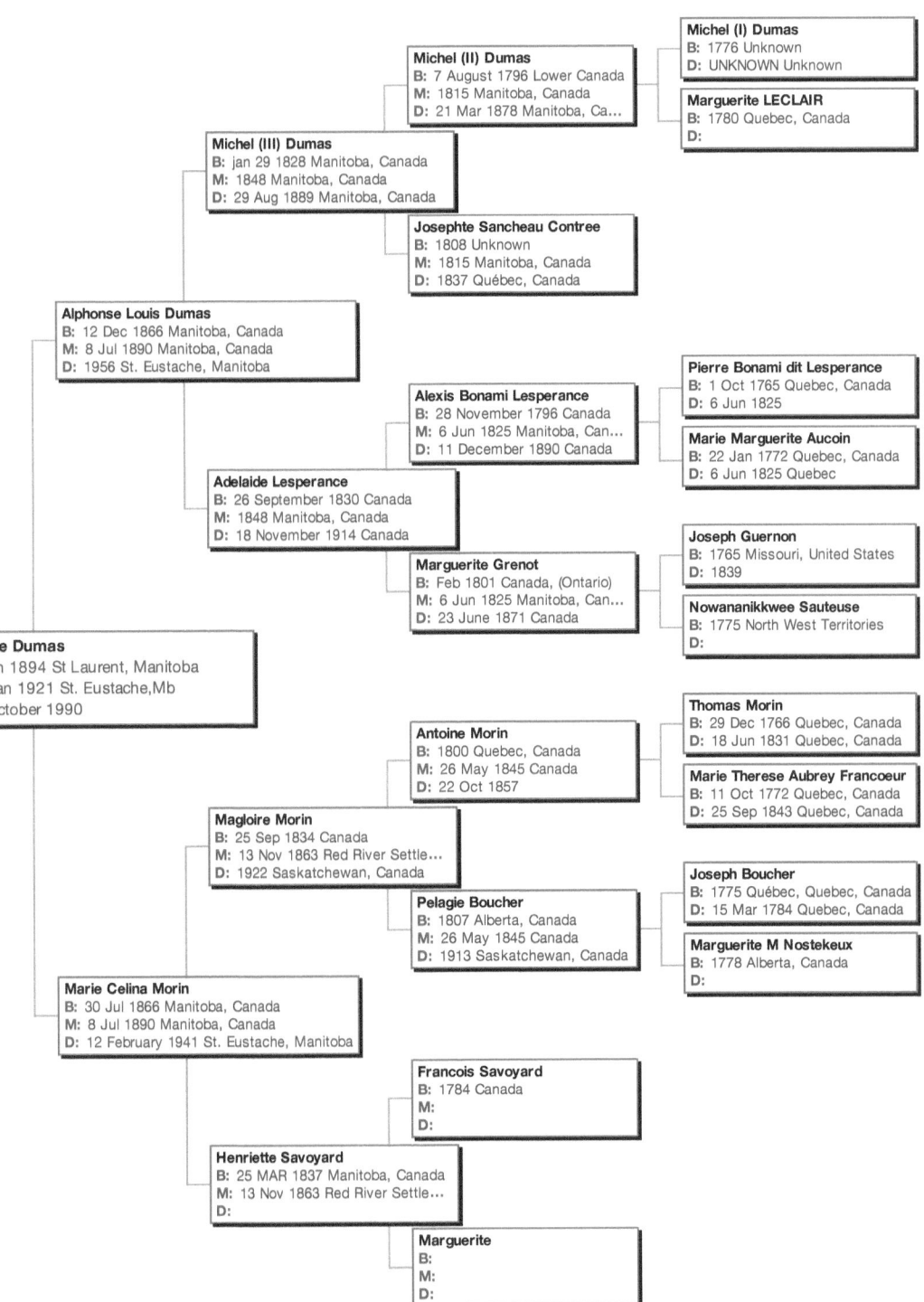

Michel (I) Dumas
B: 1776 Unknown
D: UNKNOWN Unknown

Marguerite LECLAIR
B: 1780 Quebec, Canada
D:

Michel (II) Dumas
B: 7 August 1796 Lower Canada
M: 1815 Manitoba, Canada
D: 21 Mar 1878 Manitoba, Ca...

Michel (III) Dumas
B: jan 29 1828 Manitoba, Canada
M: 1848 Manitoba, Canada
D: 29 Aug 1889 Manitoba, Canada

Josephte Sancheau Contree
B: 1808 Unknown
M: 1815 Manitoba, Canada
D: 1837 Québec, Canada

Alphonse Louis Dumas
B: 12 Dec 1866 Manitoba, Canada
M: 8 Jul 1890 Manitoba, Canada
D: 1956 St. Eustache, Manitoba

Pierre Bonami dit Lesperance
B: 1 Oct 1765 Quebec, Canada
D: 6 Jun 1825

Marie Marguerite Aucoin
B: 22 Jan 1772 Quebec, Canada
D: 6 Jun 1825 Quebec

Alexis Bonami Lesperance
B: 28 November 1796 Canada
M: 6 Jun 1825 Manitoba, Can...
D: 11 December 1890 Canada

Adelaide Lesperance
B: 26 September 1830 Canada
M: 1848 Manitoba, Canada
D: 18 November 1914 Canada

Joseph Guernon
B: 1765 Missouri, United States
D: 1839

Nowananikkwee Sauteuse
B: 1775 North West Territories
D:

Marguerite Grenot
B: Feb 1801 Canada, (Ontario)
M: 6 Jun 1825 Manitoba, Can...
D: 23 June 1871 Canada

ne Dumas
ch 1894 St Laurent, Manitoba
Jan 1921 St. Eustache,Mb
October 1990

Thomas Morin
B: 29 Dec 1766 Quebec, Canada
D: 18 Jun 1831 Quebec, Canada

Marie Therese Aubrey Francoeur
B: 11 Oct 1772 Quebec, Canada
D: 25 Sep 1843 Quebec, Canada

Antoine Morin
B: 1800 Quebec, Canada
M: 26 May 1845 Canada
D: 22 Oct 1857

Magloire Morin
B: 25 Sep 1834 Canada
M: 13 Nov 1863 Red River Settle...
D: 1922 Saskatchewan, Canada

Joseph Boucher
B: 1775 Québec, Quebec, Canada
D: 15 Mar 1784 Quebec, Canada

Marguerite M Nostekeux
B: 1778 Alberta, Canada
D:

Pelagie Boucher
B: 1807 Alberta, Canada
M: 26 May 1845 Canada
D: 1913 Saskatchewan, Canada

Marie Celina Morin
B: 30 Jul 1866 Manitoba, Canada
M: 8 Jul 1890 Manitoba, Canada
D: 12 February 1941 St. Eustache, Manitoba

Francois Savoyard
B: 1784 Canada
M:
D:

Henriette Savoyard
B: 25 MAR 1837 Manitoba, Canada
M: 13 Nov 1863 Red River Settle...
D:

Marguerite
B:
M:
D:

Alphonse Louis Dumas and Marie Celina Morin

Alphonse Louis Dumas [Metis]
Born 12 December 1866 in St. Boniface, Manitoba (at the time of birth St. Boniface was situated in the Red River Settlement). Alphonse Louis is the sixth and youngest child of Michel Dumas (III) and Adelaide Lesperance. Alphonse Louis moved from the Red River settlement to St. Laurent, Manitoba, sometime between 1881 and 1890. In 1890, Alphonse Louis married Marie Celina Morin in St. Laurent. In 1901, Alphonse Louis and his family moved to St. Francois-Xavier, Manitoba and lived in the area until his passing on 26 June, 1956 (age 89).

Marie Celina Morin [Metis]
Born 20 July, 1866 in St. Boniface, Manitoba (at the time of birth, Red River Settlement). Marie Celina is the second child of Magloire Morin and Henriette Savoyard. Marie Celina moved from St. Boniface to St. Laurent, Manitoba sometime between 1881 and 1890. Marie Celina married Alphonse Louis Dumas in 1890 in St. Laurent. Marie Celina, Alphonse Louis, and children moved to St. Francois-Xavier in 1901 and lived in the area until her passing. Marie Celine passed away 12 February, 1941 (age 74). Marie Celina held Metis Script Affidavit from her maiden family.

Siblings of Alphonse Louis Dumas

Michel Dumas (IV) (Born 1849; Married Veronique Ouellet 1875; Passed away 1901)
Further detail of the life of Michel Dumas (IV) with Michel Dumas (III)
Pierre Dumas (Born 1855; Passed away unknown)
Celina Dumas (Born 1859; Passed away unknown)
Joseph Dumas (Born 1862; Passed away unknown)

Henriette Dumas (Born 1864; Passed away unknown)

Siblings of Marie Celina Morin

Magloire (Jr.) Morin (born 1864; Passed away 1866)
Patrice Morin (Born 1868; Passed away unknown)
Louis Joseph Morin (Born 1872; Passed away 1872)
Virginie Josephine Morin (Born 1873; Passed away unknown)
Marguerite Morin (Born 1881; Passed away unknown)

Michel Dumas (III) and Adelaide Lesperance

Michel Dumas (III) [Metis]

Born 29 January, 1828 in St. Boniface in the Red River Settlement. Michel (III) comes from a large family with many siblings and half siblings. In 1848, Michel (III) married Adelaide Lesperance in St. Boniface. Between 1881 and 1889, Michel (III) moved from St. Boniface to St. Laurent, Manitoba. Michel (III) held Metis Script Affidavit.

Michel (III) was 41 years old during the Red River Rebellion of 1869. After the Manitoba Act passed in 1870 (supposing the rights of Metis people in Manitoba), The Woseley Expedition brought many White (English) settlers from Ontario west. This forced many Metis people to move and sell their Script Affidavit. Michel (III) was taken to court for falsely selling his Script twice. Michel (III) was found 'not guilty', and never did falsely sell his script.

During the 1870s, the Metis people were forced north-west due to english settlement in Manitoba. This sparked the North-West Rebellion in 1885. Michel (III) eldest son, Michel (IV), was a well known Metis resistance fighter. Michel (IV) was one of Riel's Captains during the 1869-1870 Red River Resistance. Michel (IV), along with Gabriel Dumont, was one of the four men who rode to Montana in 1885 to urge Louis Riel to return to Canada and lead his people. Michel (IV) served briefly as the secretary to Riel's governing council. Michel (IV) fought in the Battle of Duck Lake (26 March, 1885), The Battle of Fish Creek (24 April, 1885), and the Battle of Batoche (9 May, 1885) as Gabriel Dumonts right hand captain. Michel (IV) further testified for Louis Riel during Riel's trial. Michel (IV) fled to the United States after the North-West Rebellion (1885) to avoid trial from the Canadian Government. In the U.S. Dumont and Michel (IV) were arrested, only to be released two days later from instruction by President Cleveland. Michel (IV) later joined Buffalo Bills Wild West Show with his close friend Gabriel Dumont. During his time with Buffalo Bill's Wild West Show, Michel (IV) along with Maxime Goulet, Maxime Lepine, and Jules Marion were portrayed as French-Canadian trappers who rode Inuit dog sleds. Michel (IV) joined Buffalo Bill at the Paris World Fair in 1889. Michel (IV) then quit Buffalo Bills production during the world fair, and returned to Canada by telling the Canadian council in France that he was Gabriel Dumont, with the Canadian council paying for the return trip expenses.

When Michel (IV) returned to Canada from Paris, he and his family resided in Ebb and Flow reservation, on Lake Manitoba. There Michel (IV) became the first schoolteacher in the community. Michel (IV) was still wanted by the Canadian government for his role in the Northwest resistance, and oral history notes that when the police came to Ebb and Flow looking for Michel (IV), his wife, Veronique Ouellette, who was doing laundry at the time, buried him under blankets. Michel (IV) then fled to Turtle Mountain for 12 months, after which he then met with his family in St. Laurent. Michel (IV) was known as a heavy drinker, which may have contributed to his young death at the age of 52 on 13 December, 1901.

Presumably, the actions and role Michel (IV) had with the Metis resistance led Michel (III), Adelaide, and family (including Alphonse Louis) to seclude the family from persecution due to Michel (IV) involvement with Riel and Dumont. This involved a move from the Red River Settlement to the more secluded northern community of St.

Laurent. Michel (III) passed away 29 August, 1889 (age 61) in St. Laurent, Manitoba.

Adelaide Lesperance [Metis]
Born 26 September, 1830 in the Red River Settlement. Adelaide is one of many children of Alexis Bonami Lesperance and Marguerite Grenot. Under her maiden family, Adelaide held Metis Script Affidavit. In 1848, Adelaide married Michel Dumas (III) in the Red River Settlement. Adelaide moved with the family to St. Laurent sometime between 1881 and 1890. After the passing of Michel (III) Adelaide moved with her children to St. Francois Xavier in 1906. Adelaide passed away 18 November 1914 (age 84) in St. Francois-Xavier, Manitoba.

Magloire Morin and Henriette Savoyard

Magloire Morin [Metis]
Born 25 September, 1834 at Ile-a-la-Crosse, Saskatchewan. Magloire is from a family of ten children. His parents are Antoine Morin and Pelagie Boucher. Magloire married Henriette Savoyard on 13 November, 1863 in St. Boniface, Manitoba. Maglorie held Metis Script Affidavit. Magloire passed away in 1922 (age 88).

Henriette Savoyard [Metis]
Born 25 March, 1837 in St. Boniface, Red River Settlement. Henriette is the youngest child of Francois Savoyard and Marguerite (Saulteaux). Henriette married Magloire on 13 November, 1863 in St. Boniface. Henriette is a first generation Metis and held Metis Script Affidavit under her maiden family. The year of Henriette's passing is unknown.

Michel Dumas (II) and Josephte Sancheau Contree

Michel Dumas (II)
Born 7 August, 1796 in St. Ours, Sorel, Lower Canada (Present Day Quebec). Michel (II) was the first born child of Michel Dumas (I) and Margueite Leclair. Michel (II) married Josephte Sancheau Contree in 1815 in St. Boniface, Manitoba. After Josephte passed away in 1837, Michel (II) remarried in 1840 to Henriette Landry. Michel (II) held Metis Script Affidavit due to his marriage to Josephte. Michel (II) passed away 21 March, 1878 (age 81).

Josephte Sancheau Contree [Indigenous/Metis]
Born est. 1808. Her Parents and siblings are unknown. Josephte married Michel Dumas (II) in 1827 at St. Boniface, Manitoba. Josephte passed away in 1837 (age 27). For Michel (II) to hold Metis Script Affidavit under Josephte's name, Josephte would have to be of Indigenous decent (as Michel (II) is from French Settler decent). The nature of the estimation year of Josphte's birth, as well as no known family members presumes that Josphte herself is Indigenous.

Alexis Bonami Lesperance and Marguerite Grenot

Alexis Bonami Lesperance
Born 1796 in Sorel, Lower Canada. Alexis comes from a family of many children. Alexis' parents are Pierre Lesperance and Marie Aucoin. Alexis fought in the War of 1812 at the age of 16, serving in a regiment commanded by Colonel James Cuthbert. Alexis joined the Hudson Bay Company in 1816, and his contracts brought him west. In 1817, Alexis was listed at the Fort William HBC Post, Peace River District in 1818, and the Athabasca District in

1820. During his time working for the Hudson Bay Company, Alexis worked his way up the ranks. Alexis started as a voyageur, paddling and portaging the bundles being transported. Alexis then became a famed guide for the Hudson Bay Company, who may have been chosen to be the guide for George Simpsons historic canoe trip to the west coast via the Fraser River. Alexis received a promotion once again and became famous for leading the Portage La Loche brigade, noted for being the most difficult route of the Canadian fur trade. His contracts brought him to the Red River area in 1823. Alexis married Marguerite Grenot 6 June, 1825 in St. Boniface, Manitoba. Alexis was a strong supporter of Riel's actions during the Red River resistance and the Northwest Resistance. After Marguerite passed away in 1871, Alexis lived in St. Francois-Xavier. Alexis passed away 11 December, 1890 (age 94).

Marguerite Grenot [Metis]
Born February 1801 in Upper Canada (Ontario). Marguerite is the youngest child of Joseph Guernon and Nowananiikwee. Marguerite married Alexis Bonami Lesperance on 6 June, 1825 in St. Boniface, Manitoba. Marguerite is a First Generation Metis and held Metis Script Affidavit under her maiden name. Marguerite and Alexis' daughter, Caroline, married Jean Baptiste Boucher. Boucher was a member of Riel's Exovedate at Batoche. Marguerite passed away 23 June, 1871 (age 70). Her Known siblings were Joseph Little Thunder Grenon (Born 1790; Passed away 1854) and Pierre Grenon (Born 1792; Passed away unknown).

Antoine Morin and Pelagie Boucher

Antoine Morin
Born 1800 in Maskinonge, Quebec. Antoine's partents are Thomis Morin and Marie Francoeur. Antoine was a fur

trader with both the NorthWest Company and the Hudson Bay Company, bringing him west. Antoine married Pelagie Boucher 26 May, 1845 in Isle-a-la-Crosse, Saskatchewan. Antoine passed away 22 October, 1857 (age 57).

Pelagie Boucher [Metis]
Born 1807 at Peace River, Alberta, Pelagie's parents are Joseph Boucher and Marguerite Nostekeux. Pelagie married Antoine Morin on 26 May, 1845 in Isle-a-la-Crosse, Saskatchewan. Pelagie remained in the Northern Saskatchewan area until her passing in 1913 (age 106).

Francois Savoyard and Marguerite

Francois Savoyard
Born 1784. Francois' parents and siblings are unknown. Francois married Marguerite, a Saulteaux women. Dates of the marriage and of Francois' passing are unknown.

Marguerite [Ojibwe]
Born 1788. Marguerite is a Saulteaux Ojibwe women from Eastern Manitoba or Ontario. Marguerite married Francois Savoyard. Dates of the marriage and of Marguerites passing are unknown.

Michel Dumas (I) and Marguerite Leclair

Michel Dumas (I)
Born 1776 in Lower Canada. Michel (I) lived his whole life in what is now Quebec. Michel (I) parents are Louis Demer Dumas and Maire Josphte Pichet. Michel (I) married Marguerite Leclair on 19 October, 1975. Year of passing is unknown.

Marguerite Leclair
Born 1780 at Contrecoeur, Lower Canada. Marguerite's parents are Pierre Leclair and Cecil Dumas. Marguerite married Michel Dumas (I) on 19 October, 1975. Year of Passing is unknown.

Pierre Lesperance and Marie Aucoin

Pierre Lesperance
Born 1 October 1765 in Chambly, Lower Canada. Pierre's parents are Raimon Lesperance and Maire-Madeleine Thibodeau. Pierre married Maire Aucoin on 7 March, 1791 in Sorel, Lower Canada. Pierre passed away on 6 June, 1825 (age 59).

Marie Aucoin
Born 22 January, 1772 in Sorel, Lower Canada. Marie's parents are Pierre Aucoin and Marie Josephe Brisson. Marie married Pierre Lesperance on 7 March, 1791. Marie passed away 6 June, 1825 (age 53).

Joseph Guernon and Nowananikkwee

Joseph Guernon
Born 1765 in Sainte Genevieve, Missouri in the United States. Joseph's parents are Louis Grenon and Genevieve Constantino. Joseph married Nowananikkwee in 1790. Joseph passed away in 1839 (age 74).

Nowananikkwee [Ojibwe]
Born 1775 in what was considered the North West Territories (any area west of Ontario). Nowananikkwee married Joeseph Guernon in 1790 in the North West

Territories of Canada. Maternal family and year of passing is unknown.

Thomas Morin and Marie Francoeur

Thomas Morin
Born 29 December, 1766 in Neuville, Lower Canada. Thomas married Marie Francoeur on 29 September, 1788 in Maskinonge, Lower Canada. Thomas passed away 18 June, 1831 (age 64).

Marie Francoeur
Born 11 October, 1772 in Maskinonge, Lower Canada. Marie married Thomas Morin on 29 September 1788. Marie passed away on 25 September 1843 (age 70).

Joseph Boucher and Marguerite Nostekuex

Joseph Boucher
Born 1775 in Quebec City, Lower Canada. Joseph married Marguerite Nostekuex in 1790. Year of passing is unknown.

Marguerite Nostekuex [Ojibwe]
Born 1778 in Lac Ste. Anne, Alberta. Marguerite's father is Nostekuex. In 1790, Marguerite married Joseph Boucher. Year of passing is unknown.

Continuation of Michel Dumas (I) Family Tree

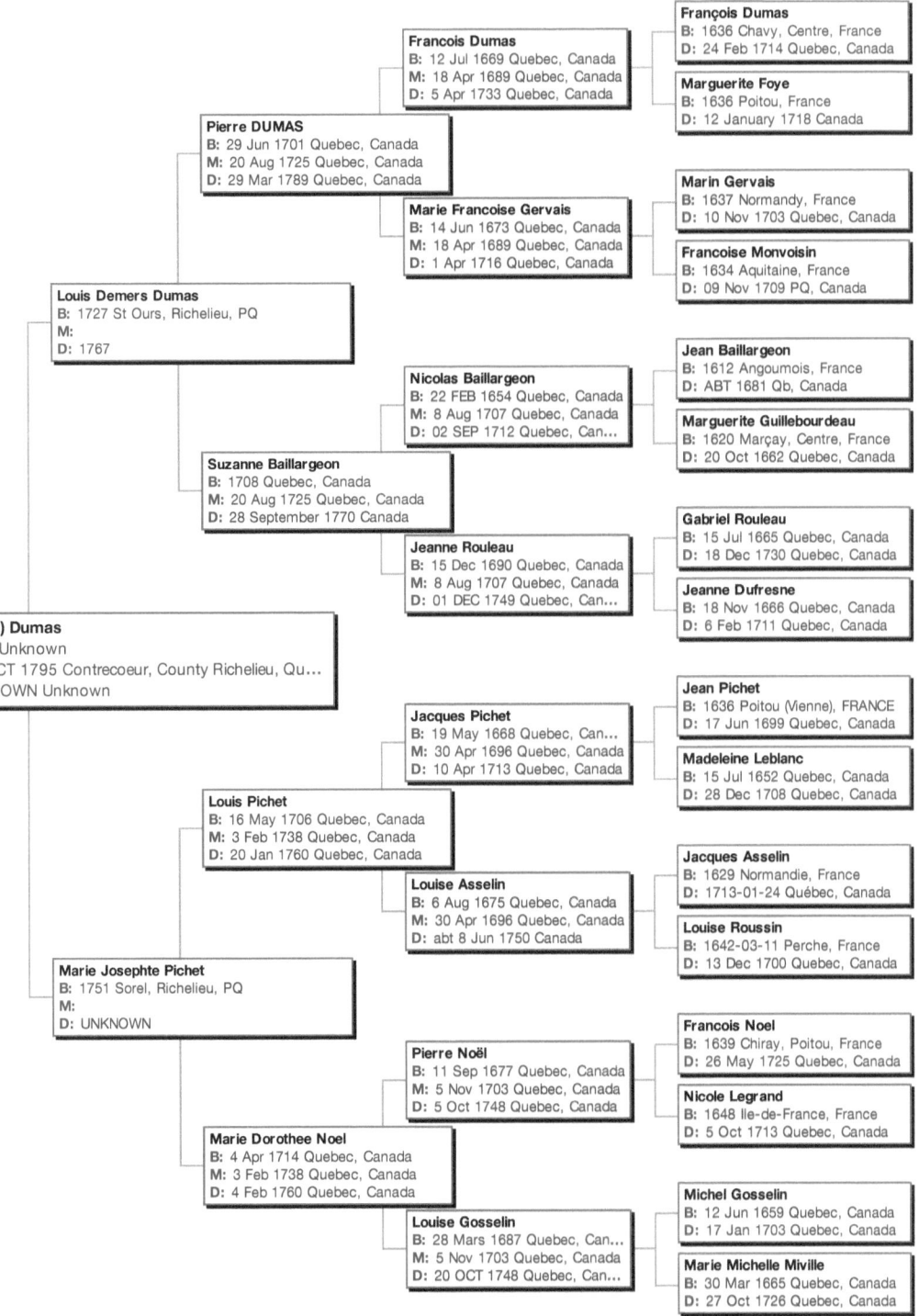

François Dumas
B: 1636 Chavy, Centre, France
D: 24 Feb 1714 Quebec, Canada

Marguerite Foye
B: 1636 Poitou, France
D: 12 January 1718 Canada

Francois Dumas
B: 12 Jul 1669 Quebec, Canada
M: 18 Apr 1689 Quebec, Canada
D: 5 Apr 1733 Quebec, Canada

Marin Gervais
B: 1637 Normandy, France
D: 10 Nov 1703 Quebec, Canada

Francoise Monvoisin
B: 1634 Aquitaine, France
D: 09 Nov 1709 PQ, Canada

Marie Francoise Gervais
B: 14 Jun 1673 Quebec, Canada
M: 18 Apr 1689 Quebec, Canada
D: 1 Apr 1716 Quebec, Canada

Pierre DUMAS
B: 29 Jun 1701 Quebec, Canada
M: 20 Aug 1725 Quebec, Canada
D: 29 Mar 1789 Quebec, Canada

Louis Demers Dumas
B: 1727 St Ours, Richelieu, PQ
M:
D: 1767

Jean Baillargeon
B: 1612 Angoumois, France
D: ABT 1681 Qb, Canada

Marguerite Guillebourdeau
B: 1620 Marçay, Centre, France
D: 20 Oct 1662 Quebec, Canada

Nicolas Baillargeon
B: 22 FEB 1654 Quebec, Canada
M: 8 Aug 1707 Quebec, Canada
D: 02 SEP 1712 Quebec, Can...

Gabriel Rouleau
B: 15 Jul 1665 Quebec, Canada
D: 18 Dec 1730 Quebec, Canada

Jeanne Dufresne
B: 18 Nov 1666 Quebec, Canada
D: 6 Feb 1711 Quebec, Canada

Jeanne Rouleau
B: 15 Dec 1690 Quebec, Canada
M: 8 Aug 1707 Quebec, Canada
D: 01 DEC 1749 Quebec, Can...

Suzanne Baillargeon
B: 1708 Quebec, Canada
M: 20 Aug 1725 Quebec, Canada
D: 28 September 1770 Canada

I (I) Dumas
?6 Unknown
OCT 1795 Contrecoeur, County Richelieu, Qu...
KNOWN Unknown

Jean Pichet
B: 1636 Poitou (Vienne), FRANCE
D: 17 Jun 1699 Quebec, Canada

Madeleine Leblanc
B: 15 Jul 1652 Quebec, Canada
D: 28 Dec 1708 Quebec, Canada

Jacques Pichet
B: 19 May 1668 Quebec, Can...
M: 30 Apr 1696 Quebec, Canada
D: 10 Apr 1713 Quebec, Canada

Jacques Asselin
B: 1629 Normandie, France
D: 1713-01-24 Québec, Canada

Louise Roussin
B: 1642-03-11 Perche, France
D: 13 Dec 1700 Quebec, Canada

Louise Asselin
B: 6 Aug 1675 Quebec, Canada
M: 30 Apr 1696 Quebec, Canada
D: abt 8 Jun 1750 Canada

Louis Pichet
B: 16 May 1706 Quebec, Canada
M: 3 Feb 1738 Quebec, Canada
D: 20 Jan 1760 Quebec, Canada

Marie Josephte Pichet
B: 1751 Sorel, Richelieu, PQ
M:
D: UNKNOWN

Francois Noel
B: 1639 Chiray, Poitou, France
D: 26 May 1725 Quebec, Canada

Nicole Legrand
B: 1648 Ile-de-France, France
D: 5 Oct 1713 Quebec, Canada

Pierre Noël
B: 11 Sep 1677 Quebec, Canada
M: 5 Nov 1703 Quebec, Canada
D: 5 Oct 1748 Quebec, Canada

Michel Gosselin
B: 12 Jun 1659 Quebec, Canada
D: 17 Jan 1703 Quebec, Canada

Marie Michelle Miville
B: 30 Mar 1665 Quebec, Canada
D: 27 Oct 1726 Quebec, Canada

Louise Gosselin
B: 28 Mars 1687 Quebec, Can...
M: 5 Nov 1703 Quebec, Canada
D: 20 OCT 1748 Quebec, Can...

Marie Dorothee Noel
B: 4 Apr 1714 Quebec, Canada
M: 3 Feb 1738 Quebec, Canada
D: 4 Feb 1760 Quebec, Canada

People of Note from Michel Dumas (I) Family Tree

Francois (Sr.) Dumas is considered to be the ancestor to the majority of Dumas French-speaking people in North America. Francois was a well known mason in the New France colony, and helped construct many of the first buildings/stone works of French Quebec. Francois married Marguerite Foye, a "Kings Daughter"

Les Dumas d'Amérique, a heritage society dedicated to the history of French-speaking Dumas' in North America, dedicated a monument in 1995 to Francois Dumas and Marguerite Foye:

"Francois and Marguerite were among the earliest French settlers of Quebec and have been designated a 'Founding Family' of New France (Quebec) and on September 24, 1995 there was a monument dedicated to them on the St. Lawrence River island, Ile de Orleans. The monument is located on the southern shore of the island, not far from where they had lived and died. It is crafted from bronze, stone masonry, and earth and is the work of sculptor Yves Bussiere and represents the corner of a wall and two bronze hands emerging from it. The muscled right hand, holding a mason's trowel, emerges from the highest corner of the wall and represents Francois's profession. The left hand emerges from the west wall in a fashion of a hand sewing seed in a new land. At the foot of the monument are three rows of planted daisies that bring to mind Francois's wife and help mate Marguerite (daisies in French are called marguerites). Near the monument are two bronze plaques, one in English and one in French"

Marguerite Foye, Francoise Monvoisin, and Nicole LeGrand all came to Canada under the "Kings Daughters" (French: *Filles du Roi*) program sponsored by King Louis XIV. The Kings Daughters program was designed to boost the new French Canadian population by promoting marriage and family formation in New France. Although other women certainly immigrated to Quebec from France before and during the program, only those who were actively recruited by the government and whose travel/immigration expenses were paid for by King Louis XIV were considered "Filles du Rois".

  Nicole LeGrand received a 450 pound dowry, a noteworthy amount, for enrolling in the Kings Daughter program. Not all women enrolled in the program received dowries, and the average of those who did receive dowries was 50 pounds.

Photographs

Above: Napoleon (Jr.) Allarie and Victorine Dumas, 1976.

Right: Hortense Allarie and Donald Schade on their wedding day, 1954.

Clockwise from Top Left: Gravesite of: Victorine Allarie (nee Dumas), Napoleon (Jr) Allarie, Napoleon (Sr) Allarie, Celina Morin (1/2), Celina Morin (2/2), Alphonse Louis Dumas, and Marie Rose Allarie (nee Piche). All found at St. Eustache Roman Catholic Cemetery

Right: The Obituaries of Napoleon Allarie (b. 1896) and Victorine Dumas (b. 1894)

Below: Pierre Allarie and Genevieve Zastre

Memorial Obituary

Entered Into Eternal Rest
Monday, Oct. 25, 1976

NAPOLEON ALLARIE

On Monday, October 25, 1976 at the St. Boniface Hospital, Napoleon Allarie, aged 80 years, beloved husband of Victorine Allarie (nee Dumas) of 328 Dussault Ave.

Besides his wife Victorine, Mr. Allarie is survived by a son Phillip of New Westminster, B.C.; six daughters, Mrs. M. Girard (Simonne), also of New Westminster, B.C., Mrs. D. Schade (Patsy) of Beausejour, Man., Mrs. Claire Tetrault, Miss Alphie Allarie, Mrs. L. Arnal (Valerie), Miss Lucie Allarie, all of Winnipeg; a sister Mrs. J. Millaire (Marie); three brothers, Gabriel, Raphael and Jean, all of St. Eustache, Man.; 30 grandchildren and 11 great-grandchildren.

Mr. Allarie was predeceased by a daughter Arthemise in 1971 and a brother Elzear in 1953.

Prayers will be said on Thursday, October 28, 1976 at 1:30 p.m. in St. Eustache Roman Catholic Church followed by Requiem Mass at 2:00 p.m. The Rev. Fr. L. Lavoie officiating. Interment in the Parish Cemetery.

The pallbearers will be the five grandsons, Edward Tetrault, James Klause, Douglas, Bruce, and Leslie Schade, and a nephew Roger Forcier.

Green Acres Memorial Chapel in care of arrangements. Phone 222-2341.

VICTORINE ALLARIE

Peacefully in her sleep at the Foyer Valade on Sunday, October 28, 1990, Victorine Allarie, aged 96 years, of Winnipeg.

She was predeceased by her husband Napoleon in 1976; one son and five daughters. She leaves to cherish her memory two daughters, Lucy Dawson and her husband Brad of Winnipeg, Patsy Schade and her husband Don of Beausejour; one sister Octavio Forcier of Winnipeg and numerous grandchildren and great-grandchildren.

The family would like to express their heartfelt thanks to the staff of Foyer Valade.

In lieu of flowers, friends may make a contribution to the Foyer Valade, 450 River Rd., Winnipeg R2M 5M4.

Prayers will be said on Thursday, November 1 at 1:30 p.m. in St. Eustache Roman Catholic Church, St. Eustache, Man., followed by the mass of christian burial also in the church. Interment to follow in the parish cemetery.

Pallbearers will be the grandsons, Douglas Schade, Paul Dawson, Thurston Helbig, Scott Skipper, Jim Klaus and Edward Tetrault.

GREEN ACRES FUNERAL CHAPEL. Ph. 222-3241.

Right: The "Allarie Ferry"; owned and operated by many members of the Allarie family. Pierre started the ferry operation, and passed down to his sons, including Napoleon (Sr.). The ferry, as seen in the picture below, transported vehicles across the Assiniboine River from St. Eustache to Baie St. Paul.

Bottom Right: Pierre Allarie standing on his ferry.

Right: Napoleon (Sr.) Allarie and Marie Rose Piche, standing with daughter Maria Millaire (middle)

Bottom Left: Sketch of Alexis Lesperance

Bottom Right: Plaque where Allarie School use to stand

Alexis L'Esperance, who commanded the Portage la Loche brigade.

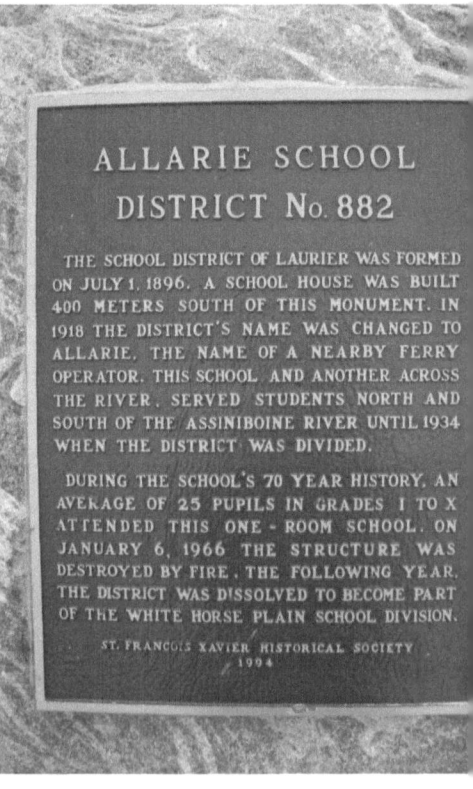

ALLARIE SCHOOL
DISTRICT No. 882

THE SCHOOL DISTRICT OF LAURIER WAS FORMED ON JULY 1, 1896. A SCHOOL HOUSE WAS BUILT 400 METERS SOUTH OF THIS MONUMENT. IN 1918 THE DISTRICT'S NAME WAS CHANGED TO ALLARIE, THE NAME OF A NEARBY FERRY OPERATOR. THIS SCHOOL, AND ANOTHER ACROSS THE RIVER, SERVED STUDENTS NORTH AND SOUTH OF THE ASSINIBOINE RIVER UNTIL 1934 WHEN THE DISTRICT WAS DIVIDED.

DURING THE SCHOOL'S 70 YEAR HISTORY, AN AVERAGE OF 25 PUPILS IN GRADES 1 TO X ATTENDED THIS ONE - ROOM SCHOOL. ON JANUARY 6, 1966 THE STRUCTURE WAS DESTROYED BY FIRE. THE FOLLOWING YEAR, THE DISTRICT WAS DISSOLVED TO BECOME PART OF THE WHITE HORSE PLAIN SCHOOL DIVISION.

ST. FRANCOIS XAVIER HISTORICAL SOCIETY 1994

MICHEL DUMAIS.

Left: Sketch of Michel Dumas (IV) (brother of Alphonse Louis Dumas), Metis resistance fighter and companion of Gabriel Dumont.
Below: Exert from Chester Brown's Louis Riel Comic Strip Biography regarding Michel Dumas (IV).

128:1

Charles Nolin had moved to the south branch of the Saskatchewan River and was one of the people who urged that a delegation be sent to Montana to meet with Riel. He was not, however, one of the four men who made the trip. The actual fourth man was named Michel Dumas.

129:3 - 130:4

Concerned that he might be

He brought me six cakes about three quarters of a pound each. These were all the provisions I took with me for a journey of 600 miles. Jean Dumont, my brother, and a few young men came to say good bye to me.

I saddled my horse, which was the best charger in Batoche, and they came with me to the edge of the wood.

I had only gone 100 yards when I heard some one shout behind me, I saw Michel Dumas, who had formerly accompanied me to Montana, when I had gone to look for Riel. He wanted to go across the line with me. He was unarmed, and he too had only a few dried cakes for provisions. We set out by the grace of God.[57]

Above: Exert from the writing of Gabriel Dumont on fleeing to the United States after the Northwest Resistance (1885). From *Metis Makers of History* by Grant MacEwan.

Top: Plaque to Francois Dumas and Marguerite Foy (sp. 'Foye') It reads "A mason and a fille du roi: on this ground sowed their fields and together, built our future."

Above: Monument to Francois Dumas and Marguerite Foye. Both the plaque and monument are in Ile d'Orleans, Quebec City, Canada and were inaugurated in 1995.

Index and References by Person

Allarie, Hortense (pg 6, 30): Canada, GenWeb Cemetery Index; Canada Obituary Collection; Personal Records.

Allarie, Napoleon (Jr.) (pg.7, 30, 31,32): 1906 Canada Census of Manitoba, Saskatchewan, and Alberta; 1916 Canada Census of Manitoba, Saskatchewan, and Alberta; 1921 Census of Canada; Canada: Soldiers of the First World War (1914-1918)

Allarie, Napoleon (Sr.) (pg. 10, 31, 34): 1891 Census of Canada; 1901 Census of Canada; 1906 Canada Census of Manitoba, Saskatchewan, and Alberta; 1916 Canada Census of Manitoba, Saskatchewan, and Alberta; 1921 Census of Canada

Allary, Michel (Sr.) (pg. 15): Quebec: Vital and Church Records (Drouin Collection 1621-1967)

Allary, Michel (pg. 14): 1861 Census of Canada; 1871 Census of Canada; Quebec: Vital and Church Records (Drouin Collection 1621-1967)

Allary, Pierre (pg. 10, 32, 33): 1891 Census of Canada; 1901 Census of Canada; 1906 Canada Census of Manitoba, Saskatchewan, and Alberta; 1911 Census of Canada; 1916 Canada Census of Manitoba, Saskatchewan, and Alberta; Canadian Genealogy index (1600-1900); Winnipeg Tribune (15 May, 1924)

Aucoin, Marie (pg. 25): Quebec: Vital and Church Records (Drouin Collection 1621-1967)

Barron, Marie (pg. 10): 1901 Census of Canada

Boucher, Joseph (pg. 26): Cyprien Morin and his Descendants

Boucher, Pelagie (pg. 24): 1851 Census of Canada East, Canada West, New Brunswick and Nova Scotia; 1861 Census of Canada; 1871 Census of Canada; 1891 Census of Canada; Cyprien Morin and his Descendants

Contre, Marie-Reine (pg. 16): Quebec: Vital and Church Records (Drouin Collection 1621-1967)

Contree, Josephte (pg. 22): Quebec: Vital and Church Records (Drouin Collection 1621-1967); 'Michel Dumas'

Dumas, Alphonse Louis (pg. 18, 31): 1881 Census of Canada; 1891 Census of Canada; 1901 Census of Canada; 1906 Canada Census of Manitoba, Saskatchewan, and Alberta; 1911 Census of Canada; 1916 Canada Census of Manitoba, Saskatchewan, and Alberta
Dumas, Francois (Sr.) (pg. 28, 36): Les Dumas d'Amérique (2014)
Dumas, Michel (I) (pg. 24): Canada Genealogy Index (1600-1900)
Dumas, Michel (II) (pg. 22): Canada Genealogy Index (1600-1900); Quebec: Vital and Church Records (Drouin Collection 1621-1967)
Dumas, Michel (III) (pg. 19): 1881 Census of Canada; Manitoba Death index (1881-1941); Veterans and Families of the 1885 Northwest Resistance.; 'Michel Dumas'
Dumas, Michel (IV) (pg. 18, 16, 35): Veterans and Families of the 1885 Northwest Resistance; Louis Riel: A comic-strip bibliography; 'Michel Dumas'; Manitowapow
Dumas, Victorine (pg. 7, 30, 31, 32): 1901 Census of Canada; 1906 Canada Census of Manitoba, Saskatchewan, and Alberta; 1911 Census of Canada; 1916 Canada Census of Manitoba, Saskatchewan, and Alberta; 1921 Census of Canada; Manitoba Marriage index (1879-1931); Quebec: Vital and Church Records (Drouin Collection 1621-1967)
Gaudin, Marie (pg. 15): Quebec: Vital and Church Records (Drouin Collection 1621-1967)
Grenot, Marguerite (pg. 23): Canada Genealogy Index (1600-1900); 'Marguerite Grenon'
Guernon, Joseph (pg. 25): Canada Genealogy Index (1600-1900)
Forcier, Lisette (pg. 16): Quebec: Vital and Church Records (Drouin Collection 1621-1967); 1861 Census of Canada; Canadian Genealogy index (1600-1900)
Foye, Marguerite (pg. 29, 26, 36): Les Dumas d'Amérique (2014); *A list of the Daughters and their husbands*
Francoeur, Marie (pg. 26): Cyprien Morin and his Descendants

LeClaire, Marguerite (pg. 25): Canada Genealogy Index (1600-1900)

LeGrand, Nicole (pg. 29): *A list of the Daughters and their husbands;*

Lesperance, Adelaide (pg. 21): 1861 Census of Canada; 1881 Census of Canada; 1906 Canada Census of Manitoba, Saskatchewan, and Alberta; 1911 Census of Canada; Manitoba Death index (1881-1941); 'Michel Dumas'; 'Marguerite Grenon'

Lesperance, Alexis Bonami (pg. 22, 34): Canada Genealogy Index (1600-1900); 1881 Census of Canada; Canadian Immigrant Records (part one); Quebec: Vital and Church Records (Drouin Collection 1621-1967); 'Marguerite Grenon'; Dictionary of Canadian Biography Vol. XI (1881-1890)

Lesperance, Pierre (pg. 25): Quebec: Vital and Church Records (Drouin Collection 1621-1967)

Nostekuex, Marguerite (pg. 26): Cyprien Morin and his Descendants

Nowananikkwee (pg. 25): Canada Genealogy Index (1600-1900)

Marie Piik-siik-sii-na (pg. 14): 1861 Census of Canada; 1871 Census of Canada; Quebec: Vital and Church Records (Drouin Collection 1621-1967)

Marguerite (pg. 24): Canadian Genealogy index (1600-1900)

Monvoisin, Francoise (pg. 29): *A list of the Daughters and their husbands*

Morin, Antoine (pg. 23): Cyprien Morin and his Descendants

Morin, Magloire (pg. 21): Cyprien Morin and his Descendants

Morin, Marie Celina (pg. 18, 31): 1881 Census of Canada; 1891 Census of Canada; 1901 Census of Canada; 1906 Canada Census of Manitoba, Saskatchewan, and Alberta; 1916 Canada Census of Manitoba, Saskatchewan, and Alberta

Morin, Thomas (pg. 26): Cyprien Morin and his Descendants

Parisien, Angelique (pg. 15): 1891 Census of Canada; 1901 Census of Canada; Canadian Genealogy index (1600-1900)

Parisien, Jean Baptiste (pg. 16): Quebec: Vital and Church Records (Drouin Collection 1621-1967); 1861 Census of Canada; Canadian Genealogy index (1600-1900)

Piche, Edward (pg. 10): 1901 Census of Canada

Piche, Marie Rose (pg. 10, 31, 34): 1891 Census of Canada; 1901 Census of Canada; 1906 Canada Census of Manitoba, Saskatchewan, and Alberta; 1916 Canada Census of Manitoba, Saskatchewan, and Alberta; 1921 Census of Canada

Savoyard, Francois (pg. 24) : Canadian Genealogy index (1600-1900)

Savoyard, Henriette (pg. 21): 1861 Census of Canada; 1906 Canada Census of Manitoba, Saskatchewan, and Alberta; 1911 Census of Canada; Canadian Genealogy index (1600-1900)

Zace, Jean (pg. 16): Quebec: Vital and Church Records (Drouin Collection 1621-1967)

Zastre, Louis Gonzague (pg. 15): 1891 Census of Canada; 1901 Census of Canada; Canadian Genealogy index (1600-1900)

Zastre, Genevieve (pg. 14, 32): 1891 Census of Canada; 1901 Census of Canada; 1906 Canada Census of Manitoba, Saskatchewan, and Alberta; 1911 Census of Canada; 1916 Canada Census of Manitoba, Saskatchewan, and Alberta; Canadian Genealogy index (1600-1900); Winnipeg Tribune (15 May, 1924)

Other References

Arnault, Laurence. *Cyprien Morin and his Descendants.* 2009.

Barkwell, Lawrence. *Marguerite Grenon.* 2014.

Barkwell, Lawrence. *Michel Dumas.* 2014.

Barkwell, Lawrence. *Veterans and Families of the 1885 Northwest Resistance.* 2009.

Brown, Chester. *Louis Riel: A comic strip bibliography.* 2003.

Les Dumas d'Amérique. 2014.

Sinclair, Niigaanwewidam James & Cariou, Warren. *Manitowapow.* 2011.

Therriault, Andre. *A list of the Daughters and their husbands.* 2010.

and a special thanks to all the work done by the Gabriel Dumont Institute of Native Studies and Applied Research, as well as the Manitoba Historical Society.